JOHN CAREY

The 1982 Booker McConnell Prize Speech

faber and faber

Published by Faber and Faber Limited
3 Queen Square London WC1N 3AU
Printed in Great Britain by The John Roberts Press
Clerkenwell Green, London EC1

Publication has been made possible by
the generosity of Booker McConnell.
The author's and publisher's receipts
are being donated to the National Book League.

British Library Cataloguing in Publication Data

Carey, John
The 1982 Booker McConnell Prize speech.
I. Title
825'.914 PR6062.E33

ISBN 0-571-13106-9

Professor John Carey, the chairman of the judges for the 1982 Booker McConnell Prize, delivered the following speech at the presentation dinner in Stationers' Hall, London, on 19 October.

The other judges were Paul Bailey, Frank Delaney, Janet Morgan and Lorna Sage.

The Booker McConnell Prize is an annual award of £10,000 given to the author of the best eligible novel, in the opinion of the judges, published each year. It was first given in 1969.

The 1982 prize was awarded to Thomas Keneally for his novel *Schindler's Ark*. The short list also included *Silence Among the Weapons* by John Arden, *An Ice-Cream War* by William Boyd, *Constance or Solitary Practices* by Lawrence Durrell, *The 27th Kingdom* by Alice Thomas Ellis and *Sour Sweet* by Timothy Mo.

The prize is sponsored by Booker McConnell and administered by the National Book League.

One thing a literary critic must be able to recognize is an anti-climax. After the excitements of the last hour I have a strong sense that an anti-climax is what I am going to involve you all in now, and for that reason this speech will not be exceptionally long. But it would be demeaning, both to the Booker McConnell prize and to the ninety authors whose books have been submitted for judgement this year, not to say something clear and definite about the prize itself and about how the judges reached their decision.

We live in a relative universe. No one believes in absolute judgements any more. We generally agree that judgement in artistic matters is in part culturally determined—a product of the judge's education and background—and in part subjective, answering to the judge's peculiar set of psychological needs. For those authors who have not won the Booker prize this year, these thoughts should provide some consolation.

It might seem that in this situation literary prizes are obsolete—like mastodons or mammoths: survivors from a bygone age of critical absolutism. In fact, I think, just the opposite is true. It's precisely because literary judgements have been cut loose from certainty that a public act of considered judgement, such as the Booker judges undertake each year, acquires a new usefulness. It acts as an incitement, a spur, a provocation. It forces public re-assessment of what our criteria for literature are: what kind of fiction, what kind of storybook world we choose to give house-room to in our minds, and why. The arguments which regularly surround the Booker prize, however sophisticatedly phrased, come down in the end to these rather simple and puzzling questions. And these questions matter because the answers we give to them are instrumental in deciding what kind of people we are and what kind of culture we have.

The imaginative energies of a culture appear, of course, in the whole mass of fictions that it spins—running from its jokes to its journalism, from its politics to its commercials. We recognize novels, though, as a distinct branch of this fantasizing activity, with unusual claims to power, prestige and independence. But what use are novels? What good do they do? Is it worth keeping the novel form alive? The best sort of answer to those questions (or the answer that will best suit the kind of person likely to ask them) is to point out that the life of the imagination is not just a holiday, a relaxation, but a necessary precondition for thought. Thought, in any real sense, cannot take place unless the imagination is alive. Thought needs the imagination as the context within which it operates.

Consequently you can't have a thinking culture unless you have an imagining one. If you take, for example, the connection between the movement for social reform in the nineteenth century and the novels in which the imaginative context of that movement was created, you can see a particularly clear instance of the way in which fiction can be a dynamic, thought-promoting activity within a culture—not only educating the heart, as great novels always have, but also extending the capacity of the communal mind.

From what I have said you will have gathered that I believe the relations between art and life, however various, oblique and elusive, to be a vital element in literature. In the modern debate about this point both sides, I think, have misrepresented their opponent's position, and sometimes their own as well. The idea that narrative is purely self-referential understandably frightens and infuriates conservatives. But the proposition that narrative can teach us, among other things, about narrative is surely healthy, and one of the novel's proper functions. And in teaching us about narrative it must teach us about life. For turning life into narrative is one of our basic human activities. It is the only way we can render life understandable. We turn ourselves and our pasts into narratives in order to apprehend them.

Theoretical points of this kind did not, you may be relieved to hear, occupy the judges much. Reading a lot of novels very quickly impresses on you the truth that there are basically only two types of novel, those which are well written and those which aren't. There's nothing that can be done to redeem the latter kind, however well meaning, worthy or 'experimental' they may be. The distinction between the traditional and the experimental novel is, in any case, too crude to be of use. For a genuine writer, every sentence is an experiment. Contrariwise, a novel doesn't become experimental in any gainful sense by virtue of having, say, three endings or large spaces between its paragraphs. It may merely be feeble, pretentious or indecisive. Those who imagine that there is something called the traditional novel, which aims at something simple called realism, are plainly out of touch with the immense variety of kinds of interaction between fiction and reality which the novel has developed during its history.

The novelist's function, whatever kind he chooses, is to renew life for us, to make it more interesting, more unexpected, more valuable, and to do that by seeing it more acutely than we could have done without him. Of course, this may make his own life difficult at times. There's a story about Arnold Bennett, who was boasting to Hugh Walpole about how well he had written the death of Darius Clayhanger in the Clayhanger trilogy. 'That lingering death', said Bennett, 'could scarcely be bettered. And why? Because I took infinite pains over it. All the time my father was dying, I was at the bedside making copious notes. You can't just slap these things down. You have to take trouble.'

Another thing the novelist has to take trouble over is not losing his audience. The unease which surrounds the development of the novel in our century hinges on the feeling that the mass audience is unfit to have literature written for it, and that quality writing must therefore become more and more of a minority interest, like handloom weaving or crochet work. The doctrines preached by the Modernists in the 1920s and 1930s encouraged this intellectual snobbery. By the cultivation of obscurity, and importations of esoteric knowledge, modern writing was designedly rendered unattractive to the majority of the population.

Looking at our culture now, we can see the damage which these socially and educationally divisive practices have brought about. The basic error of the modernist ethos now seems sadly obvious. For if the function of literature is to foster imaginative sympathy, then should not the writer, of all people, set an example by having enough imaginative sympathy with his audience to gain and keep their attention? Imaginative sympathy is hardly likely to be fostered by someone who feels he is too good to write for the majority of his fellow men.

Among the many reasons there are for being glad about the Booker prize, the major one, to my mind, is the publicity that surrounds it, because that is what attracts new readers and swells the audience for modern fiction. It helps to break down the barrier between the ordinary reader and contemporary writing which half a century of Modernism has painstakingly built up. From this viewpoint, too, the extraordinary diversity of the ninety novels entered this year—the variety of kinds, modes, styles, subjects—though at first it seemed (to me, anyway) bewildering and chaotic, emerges as a strength. Of course, you can envisage a doctrinaire approach to the novel which would impose a more uniform pattern. The approved prototype would follow certain avant garde academic recipes; whereas there would be a strict embargo on a kind of novel which English writers have periodically succeeded at since the time of Jane Austen—namely, subtle and unstrident social comedy through which the reader is sensitized to the intricacies of human behaviour. There have been several novels of this sort entered this year, by Anita Brookner, William Cooper, Penelope Lively and A. N. Wilson; and a brilliant one by Alice Thomas Ellis appears in the short list. At all events, the English novel is happily refusing to conform to any set model, to judge from the Booker entries. They seemed to cater for every conceivable species of reader—as well as some inconceivable ones.

That brings me to a word of complaint. The judges found themselves at a loss to understand how any publisher could have believed that some of the novels submitted this year could come within a million miles of the Booker prize. Surely a novel must have, to qualify, some semblance of being a serious and competent attempt at literary art? If it hasn't, entering it merely wastes the judges' already very limited time, and that benefits no one.

But what about the novels by authors who, on any publisher's reckoning, might rightly expect to qualify for a short list and who, this year, didn't? There was Anthony Burgess's *The End of the World News*, prodigiously inventive, like everything Burgess writes, and cramming into its huge, swaying superstructure a life of Sigmund Freud, the lyrics for a musical about Trotsky and a full scenario for the destruction of life on our planet. Parts of this novel were better written than anything else I read this year, but big sections of it take themselves extremely easily, and leave it half-accomplished. On a smaller scale, John Fowles's *Mantissa* executed some dazzlingly artful tricks, but behind the virtuosity it had, it seemed to me, nothing to transmit except flippancy and self-regard. Alan Sillitoe's *Her Victory* was really three novels—one of them a skilful but incongruous pastiche of Conrad dealing with seafaring life. It seemed sheer chance that had brought the three plots together, and as the design disintegrated, so did the ideas and the feelings. David Storey's *A Prodigal Child* also suffered from design faults. The early part, about the disadvantaged son of a farm labourer, was penetrating and poignant in the *Sons and Lovers* tradition. But when the boy goes on to have an affair with his wealthy benefactress he no longer seems the same person, or any person. He seems a novelistic proposition, and his alleged artistic gifts are not corroborated by anything we see of his creative mind.

These four are, I suppose, the obvious big excluded names. But there are several other writers, some well-known, who have added notably to the richness of this year's entry. Judy Allen's *December Flower* is a generous, witty novel about caring for the aged. This is one of the few really new twentieth-century subjects: modern medicine's gift to the novelist, as it were, to make up for the elimination of infant mortality which was such a standby in nineteenth-century fiction. The most purely cheering book I read this year was Ursula Bentley's *The Natural Order*, her first novel, and an extremely funny investigation of love and lechery in the sixth form. Belonging together as evocations of rural life were Bruce Chatwin's *On the Black Hill* and Iain Crichton Smith's *A Field Full of Folk*. Chatwin's documentary manner has the disadvantage of leaving his central characters relatively unexplored. They tend to be presented, rather, as meritorious specimens. But the book has a rare quality of spiritual depth, and so has the Crichton Smith. *A Field Full of Folk* is a poet's novel which uses events as ordinary as a wheelbarrow race at a Sunday school sports day to introduce a luminous religious vision. Modern readers embarrassed by religion will naturally find it offensive. I thought it profound and moving. Another novel guaranteed to divide readers was Lisa St Aubin de Terán's *Keepers of the House*. Its relentless emphasis on cruelty, torment, famine, massacre and corporal disfigurement will seem merely gloating to some, but powerfully disturbing to others.

I must not try your patience by keeping on about the novels we haven't even managed to fit on to the short list, but I shall risk mentioning two others briefly, because I enjoyed them a lot and they haven't received much attention. These are Stephen Benatar's *Wish Her Safe at Home* and David Batchelor's *Children in the Dark*. Mr Benatar's book is about a lonely spinster going quietly and genteelly crazy, and it involves you so strongly that you begin to feel horribly embarrassed about the impression you realize she must be making on the other characters. David Batchelor's novel is a black comedy, acute, witty, desolating, centring on an act of incest between father and daughter, but really about varieties of betrayal and human loss. My fellow judges were smilingly tolerant but unconvinced by my enthusiasm for this book, so I'd like some of you to try it and see if you agree with me or them.

And so to the short list. You could hardly find six novels with less in common, and that reflects the diversity of the whole entry. Alice Thomas Ellis's *The 27th Kingdom* I've touched on already as exemplifying the central strengths of English social comedy—astringent, intelligent, terse, perceptive. It's more than all these, of course, since it incorporates a religious dimension in the person of the novice nun Valentine, who levitates, flies and performs miracles. The beautifully poised tone of the book comes from the way it aligns religion with wit, with gladness, with something as natural as laughter. It glistens with elegance and precision like the inside of a watch. Of course, these graces preclude their opposites. In order to rise so sparklingly, religion has to be emptied of some of its weight. I feel a bit uneasy, too, as I often do in the novels of Muriel Spark, about the crushing distinction that seems to be made between the vulgar on the one hand and the saved on the other. These qualms don't detract much, though, from my admiration for its pungency, its silken ironies: it's a masterly performance.

'Masterly' is a word used so often about Lawrence Durrell that he must be tired of hearing it, and *Constance or Solitary Practices* seems to me to contain not only a lot that is typically sumptuous, but also some of his most incisive writing. The study of the German general Von Esslin opens up for us the arid hinterland of a personality, so that this character hangs like a dark weight at the fiction's centre. By contrast, the theorizing elsewhere about sexuality, oxygen, fictiveness and so on seemed to me to stay at an explanatory level.

Timothy Mo's *Sour Sweet*, about a Chinese family living in London, is, like many of its characters, guilefully unpretentious, but it achieves something very difficult in that it shows us a culture that's quite beyond our grasp, yet makes us feel we grasp it enough to share the obliquities of the immigrant's experience—like viewing ourselves and our normal surroundings through twisted glass. The portraits of the wife Lily and her sister, and of Lily's son, are rare feats of wry, off-key insight and restraint. It's a novel I'm particularly pleased to have on the short list, because I think that it might, through underplaying itself, have been missed.

John Arden's *Silence Among the Weapons* is a panoramic historical novel which triumphs by not seeming historical at all. A whole repertoire of devices—like the colloquial names used to disguise the classical figures—removes the pastness of the past and displaces the dignity and purpose which history tends to acquire by being put into books. The eternal human verities such as massacre, rape, terrorism, espionage and power-lust are set against the fragile makeshifts of art, as represented by the down-at-heel actor-manager Ivory. The theme, as Lorna Sage put it in one of our judging sessions, is how art can survive in an age that is obsessed by the spectacle of its own violence. You can't have anything more contemporary than that.

William Boyd's *An Ice Cream War* is obviously a compellingly entertaining read, and that will count against it with critics who believe that novels should ideally repel readers. Its imaginative reconstruction of the African campaign is meticulous, bizarre, captivating, but its themes are serious and contemporary. It shows individuals following their personal, isolating, absurd codes and obsessions, often self-destructively, in a universe geared to nothing more helpful than ironic mischance and the inescapable, humiliating disintegration of the human body. The humour is not incidental but integral, exemplifying a stance which, though it cannot alter this tragic vision, can make it more bearable without, at the same time, sacrificing feeling. Boyd combines seriousness with popularity, as the novel must if it is to live. In this, as in other respects—not least that he is, at 30, the youngest of the short-listed authors with, one hopes, many novels still inside him—it is an exhilarating achievement.

About Thomas Keneally's *Schindler's Ark* there's been some public debate: is it really fiction? We're used by now, though, to novels that build themselves out of facts. It's a logical conclusion of realism, and also a natural self-protecting strategy for the novel in an age overloaded with newsprint, newsfilm and documentation. We're used, too, to the realization that history is, anyway, always a kind of fiction—at best a version of and selection from a totality that can never be known. Keneally shuns make-believe, and that seems the only honourable course, given the magnitude of the tragedy he has to relate. But he still has to order and mould his material as any novelist must. He still has to take a multitude of imaginative decisions about viewpoint, emphasis, the interior and exterior of characters. It seems to us that Keneally opens a door. He makes certain possibilities imaginable, which we have too easily said are unimaginable. His book has behind it a powerful organizing and speculative mind, exercising great tact and restraint in the presentation of its terrible story. The central character, Schindler, is left in the middle distance, only half-known, as human beings are, yet dramatically present.

I have gone on too long. I'm reminded of a story told about Dylan Thomas, who was holding forth at great length one day in a sunny field above Newlyn, refreshing himself occasionally from a bottle of tonic wine which he had bought from a Penzance herbalist. Suddenly Thomas stopped talking. 'Somebody's boring me,' he said. 'I think it's me.'

But before I sit down I must record my warmest thanks to my fellow judges—Janet, Lorna, Frank and Paul—for teaching me so much and putting up with me so patiently; to Michael Caine and Booker McConnell for making this whole thing possible; to the novelists for giving me an unforgettable, if exhausting, summer; and to you all for listening. Thank you.

Previous winners of the Booker McConnell Prize

1969 *Something to Answer for* by P. H. Newby (Faber & Faber)
1970 *The Elected Member* by Bernice Rubens (Eyre Methuen)
1971 *In A Free State* by V. S. Naipaul (Deutsch)
1972 *G* by John Berger (Weidenfeld & Nicolson)
1973 *The Siege of Krishnapur* by J. G. Farrell (Weidenfeld & Nicolson)
1974 *The Conservationist* by Nadine Gordimer (Cape) *joint winner*
1974 *Holiday* by Stanley Middleton (Hutchinson) *joint winner*
1975 *Heat and Dust* by Ruth Prawer Jhabvala (John Murray)
1976 *Saville* by David Storey (Cape)
1977 *Staying On* by Paul Scott (Heinemann)
1978 *The Sea, The Sea* by Iris Murdoch (Chatto & Windus)
1979 *Offshore* by Penelope Fitzgerald (Collins)
1980 *Rites of Passage* by William Golding (Faber & Faber)
1981 *Midnight's Children* by Salman Rushdie (Cape)